What Research  Says to the Teacher

Parent-Teacher Conferencing

by Joseph C. Rotter
   Edward H. Robinson III

nea PROFESSIONAL LIBRARY
National Education Association
Washington, D.C.

WITHDRAWN

Note

The opinions expressed in this publication should not be construed as representing the policy or position of the National Education Association. Materials published as part of the What Research Says to the Teacher series are intended to be discussion documents for teachers who are concerned with specialized interests of the profession.

Library of Congress Cataloging in Publication Data

Rotter, Joseph C.
  Parent-teacher conferencing.

  (What research says to the teacher)
  Bibliography: p.
  1. Parent-teacher conferences.
  1. Robinson, E. H. (Edward H.) II. Title.
III. Series.
LC225.5R67. 1982   371.1'03   82-12428
ISBN 0-8106-1057-4

CONTENTS

The Authors

Joseph C. Rotter is Professor and Chairperson in the Department of Counselor Education and Rehabilitation Services at the University of South Carolina, Columbia. A former high school teacher and counselor at the elementary, junior and senior high school levels, he is a contributor to professional journals and coauthor of *Significant Influence People: A SIP of Discipline and Encouragement.*

Edward H. Robinson III is an Assistant Professor in the College of Education at the University of South Carolina. A former public school teacher, counselor, and administrator, he has also written, researched, and consulted on the parent-teacher conference, teacher communication skills, and teacher-student interactions in the classroom.

The Advisory Panel

Kathleen W. Corrao, sixth grade teacher, Brookfield El mentary School, Vermont

Jennie C. Ellis, English instructor and Education Specialist, Henry Ford II High School, Sterling Heights, Michigan

Ronald Peter Eydenberg, teacher, Revere High School, Massachusetts

Donald D. Megenity, Department of Psychology, University of Southern Colorado, Pueblo

Eula Ewing Monroe, Associate Professor of Teacher Education, Western Kentucky University, Bowling Green

Martha Stanfill, fifth grade teacher, Chaffee School, Huntsville, Alabama

Darrell L. Uphold, Assistant Principal, Uniontown Arear High School, Pennsylvania

INTRODUCTION

Mary Hinton has a student in her class who rarely completes an assignment and complains of stomach aches. Jon Bowles has a student in his class who has exceptional ability but spends a great deal of time daydreaming. Sherry Atwater tells of a student in her class who has a temper that can be ignited by the slightest spark. David Williams notes that many of his students are doing outstanding work and would like to share it with their parents.

Have you ever worried about how to handle these and similar situations and, more specifically, how to involve parents?* Have you wondered how to approach parents most effectively or how parents might react to messages from the teacher? Have you ever questioned your own adequacies in relating with parents? Many teachers have experienced such concerns. This publication is intended to help these teachers and all who would like to improve their parent-teacher conferencing skills. First, it examines the historical background and research relating to parent-teacher conferences. Then, it suggests effective ways for teachers to improve their communication skills with parents and involve parents in the educational, personal, and social development of their children.

NEED FOR EFFECTIVE PARENT-TEACHER CONFERENCING

It is well established by research that children enter school with very different skills and learning styles (9, 2, 34).** The source of these differences has been traced to environmental, behavioral, and genetic factors (2). The fact that 95 percent of the children who enter school can learn the same amount of material to the same level of difficulty may at first appear to contradict these two assumptions (9). With study, however, it becomes apparent that when these differences are taken into account in the teaching process, "equal educational outcomes" can and do occur (34). Despite this notion of equality and the obvious contributions of environment, learned behavior, and genetics, it becomes quite evident that influential as teachers are, perhaps the most influential factor in the learning process is the home environment (55). Teacher-parent cooperation, however, has been demonstrated to be an effective means of maximizing learning (5, 26, 37).

---

*The word "parent(s)" is used throughout this publication to refer to the primary caretaker, whether parent(s) or guardian(s).
**Numbers in parentheses appearing in the text refer to the Bibliography beginning on page 30.

Another reason for the need for effective parent-teacher conferencing is the continuing demand and legitimate right of parents to have a voice in the education of their child. From both legal and social perspectives, parents have become more interested in the day-to-day activities of the school. For the most part, this is a welcome development. But unless parents and teachers are open with each other, problems may arise. In order to achieve the goals of education, an effective partnership between the school and the home is imperative. When teachers and parents view the educational process as a collaborative effort, the parent-teacher conference becomes a key instructional strategy that will enhance the child's growth and promote more effective learning (35).

ROADBLOCKS AND GREEN LIGHTS

The roadblocks to effective parent-teacher conferencing are made up of the anxieties of the teacher, the parent, or both (36). As a result of these anxieties, whatever their source, needed contacts between home and school are often avoided; and, unfortunately, many unanswered school-related problems become compounded by neglect. Just as the rumor transmision process tends to distort a message, so it is with an unresolved problem. Out of fear of reprisals many teachers avoid the necessary parent contacts to deal with a problem before it becomes more serious. The irony is that one-third of these problems can be eliminated through face-to-face discussion by the parties involved.

One caution, however, is that interactions between parents and teachers can be for better or *worse*. Placing parents and teachers in the same room does not make the experience fruitful (33). Inappropriate procedures and inadequate skills and knowledge can create greater problems than may have existed before the meeting (35). This critical point alone should convince teachers of the importance of a set of appropriate skills for parent-teacher conferences (1). Teachers who acquire these skills can improve their interactions with parents. Teachers who fear the wrath of hostile parents can prepare themselves as facilitators of successful interactions with parents. Left alone, problems may go away; more than likely they will get worse. So it becomes a matter of being "condemned if you do and condemned if you don't." This publication suggests some ways to avoid the condemnation syndrome.

One of the myths of parent involvement in schools is "What they don't know won't hurt them." Another myth is "Parents do more harm than good." In isolated cases, perhaps, these notions can be and have been documented. In general and when teachers are adequately trained to work with parents the opposite is the case. In fact, the impact of parent involvement surpasses expectations.

When parents are familiar with school programs and activities, especially as they affect their children, they are less likely to become defensive or to show hostility. Parents can be the teacher's greatest allies, and when invited to become involved, they tend to become allies. When parents and teachers talk, a ripple effect occurs — that is, students become more positively involved. As parents become more aware of the school's goals, so do teachers become empathic to the home situation and the impact of the home environment on the child's success (45).

HISTORICAL FOUNDATIONS

Since the United States established an organized system of education, the premise has been that parents and teachers work toward the cooperative goal of educating children. Athough most individuals would still agree that this is a realistic appraisal of the parent-teacher relationship, in fact, many changes have evolved since the beginning of the national schooling process (55). Several important aspects deserve consideration if one is to understand the parent-teacher relationship of today. They are based in three broad areas: changes in society in general, resultant changes in organized education, and specific legislation that has affected the school and the parent-teacher relationship in particular.

David Tyack writes of a time in our history when the parent-teacher relationship was based on mutual experience as this excerpt from a teacher's diary shows:

Monday: Went to board at Mr. B.'s; had baked gander for dinner; suppose from its size, the thickness of the skin and other venerable appearances it must have been one of the first settlers of Vermont; made a slight impression on the patriarch's breast. Supper — cold gander and potatoes. Family consists of the man, good wife, daughter Peggy, four boys, Pompey the dog, and a brace of cats. Fire built in the square room about nine o'clock, and a pile of wood lay by the fireplace; saw Peggy scratch her fingers, and couldn't take the hint; felt squeamish about the stomach, and talked of going to bed; Peggy looked sullen, and put out the fire in the square room; went to bed and dreamed of having eaten a quantity of stone wall. (56)

Even through the turn of the century and into the first half of the twentieth century, this common experience level was high. The complete dependency of the teacher was perhaps not as intense or as traceable as it had been in earlier history, but for the most part teachers and parents shared a community focus. They lived in the same neighborhoods and attended many of the same social events, so that communication between them was facilitated by the neighborhood concept (49).

Changes Affecting Parent-Teacher Relationships

Although many changes occurred in society before the midpoint of this century, they are almost like a train. At first, as the wheels spin on the tracks, the train seems to take forever to start, but once started the speed accelerates, not at a constant rate but proportionately greater with each new click and clack of the wheels. So it seems with social changes. The great rush to the population centers, the great advances in technology that affect every part of the social structure, increased leisure time, increased affluence, increased mobility, television, space exploration — all remind the observer of the breakneck speed with which society's train has been moving in this century. As these technological changes have occurred, their impact on the social structure has been considerable. For example, the family unit changed, first from the extended family into the nuclear family and then into a number of different-type units such as the one-parent family (which in 1976 reported 7,242,000 single female heads of household) (15).

These changes in society were quickly reflected by the schools. As the population became more centralized, so did the schools. Consolidation occurred not only as a result of *Brown* v. *the Board of Education of Topeka, Kansas,* but also as a result of rural schools losing vast numbers of students and new urban schools becoming overcrowded. The mobility of populations increased and the complexion of neighborhoods changed as they experienced immigration, migration, and assimilation patterns. The combined results yielded schools with teachers and parents moving in and out, coming from diverse backgrounds, and often living in communities many miles apart. No longer do parent and teacher share a sense of common experience, nor are the opportunities to interact on a day-to-day basis an integral part of home-school life (49, 50). This unintentional wedge between teacher and parent has created a gap that many researchers feel must be filled (20, 28, 33).

Because of the loss of firsthand experiences shared by parents and teachers, communication becomes a process that must be fostered, not just allowed to happen (40, 41). This has been the underlying principle of recent legislative efforts at both the national and local levels (50, 54). For example, Public Law 94-142 and ESEA Title I have stressed the collaborative role of parents and teachers in the educational process (50). Much of the literature has heralded the intent if not the actual legislation (50). Indeed, the current literature repeatedly stresses the need and possible benefits of increased parental involvement (5, 14, 28, 29, 33, 35, 40, 44).

In recent years another perhaps more negative rationale for better cooperation between parents and teachers has come to the forefront. Increasing criticism of the schools for not teaching the basics, for being havens for teaching secular humanism, for undermining parental rights has been more prevalent (39). Such charges often stem from hard times and eras of great social change. As an institution readily accessible to the public, the schools must be prepared to deal with criticism, but they are an easier target if parents are not involved (39). When meaningful communication and collaboration is occurring between parents and teachers, such charges do not hold the attention of the school patrons; when parents feel alienated or isolated, however, irrepressible and unfounded criticisms grow out of proportion (39).

The need for effective communication between teachers and parents is clear. Although many roadblocks exist, the mutual benefits of cooperation outweigh the obstacles. The historical roots for a collaborative relationship are strong, but changes over time require that teachers discover new ways to revive that relationship. Certainly the current support for increased teacher-parent contact is evident and the current social pressures on the schools can be handled through effective parent-teacher interaction in the conference.

INTERPERSONAL COMMUNICATION SKILLS

At the heart of effective parent-teacher conferences specifically and the parent-teacher relationship in general are interpersonal communication skills. "Communication . . . is the key to good home-school relations" (7) and "the parent-teacher conference is the most direct and most meaningful mode of communication between the home and the school" (32). There seems to be a consensus in the literature that in one way or another communication skills are the essential elements that determine the success or failure of the conference (26, 32, 35, 40). It should also be noted that many researchers have pointed out the lack of attention paid to assisting teachers in developing their conferencing skills in either pre-service or in-service education (43, 44).

Ideally, the maximum benefits result when both parents and teachers have adequate interpersonal communication skills and come together to meet whatever goal may be essential to a child's continued growth and development. However, most educators are used to less than ideal situations. Although parents know what constitutes a meaningful parent-teacher conference and often have constructive suggestions for this end (32), the burden for success falls upon the teacher (14, 26, 35, 47). This is not to suggest that the teacher is to blame for a conference that goes awry. Parents often bring to an interview with the teacher a number of hidden agendas — frustrations from their own school experiences, unsuccessful past conferences, or personal concerns or problems that interfere with any meaningful process that may occur in a conference with even the most skilled and concerned teacher (36). It is reasonable to assume, however, that of the two parties involved, the teacher is in a position to control more intervening variables that inhibit productive conferences (41). Furthermore, the teacher is the paid professional in the relationship whose job, in part, is to seek ways to promote the success of the child in the educational process, and effective parent-teacher relationships have demonstrated this outcome (40, 43, 50, 55). To the extent that the teacher is knowledgeable concerning the general characteristics of effective conferences and has the interpersonal skills necessary to promote effective communication within the conference structure, the chances for success are greatly increased (35, 41, 49). A later section of this publication deals at length with the general conference characteristics. This section addresses the heart of the conference itself — the communication skills. First, it addresses the global elements identified in the literature as essential to effective communication in the interview setting; then it focuses on the specific skills and elements involved.

In reference to the parent conference, Ostrom states that "to do well in communicating we must count on relating to others with an attitude characterized by trust, openness, and hopefulness" (41). Losen and Diament stress the "need to show genuine respect for the parents' point of view" and the need for the teacher to remain "nonjudgmental" when addressing the parents' attitudes and values and to be "empathetic, i.e., to try to identify with and respond to the feelings the parents might have about coming in for the conference" (37). Prichard stresses the need for teachers to be aware of the possible defensiveness of the parent(s) in communicating with them. In a major study involving 400 teachers in urban settings, Prichard concludes that the majority of these educators felt better about their conferencing abilities after receiving some training in specific skills that provide open communication (43). Birnie indicated that the teacher needs to communicate in a nonauthoritarian way that shows understanding, empathy, and caring (7).

The literature on communication skills in parent-teacher conferences, although limited, shows a direct relationship to that body of knowledge sometimes referred to as human relations development skills. At its core are those skills which have been demonstrated to provide positive outcomes for a wide variety of human interactions. The base of these skills is communication. This body of knowledge has been successfully applied to the business world, medical science, and education (3, 11, 23, 45). A number of authors have noted the importance of the general interpersonal communication skills contained in human relations development models as they relate to the parent-teacher conference (1, 43, 49). Although many models exist, most suggest that there are certain conditions which the teacher must communicate to have a positive effect in a conference. These conditions include warmth, empathy, respect, concreteness, genuineness, self-disclosure, immediacy, and confrontation (21, 24, 45). Their presence has led to positive outcomes in the parent conference (43, 49). They are conveyed through skills than can be learned (51, 58, 59), including listening, attending, perceiving, responding, and initiating (22, 24). If these conditions and skills are important in the interpersonal communication process, it is necessary to understand their meaning when applied to the specific context of the parent-teacher conference.

Conditions of Effective Communication

Warmth is caring for the person as an individual. It denotes neither approval nor disapproval of any particular action, but rather a valuing of the individual as a person (22, 24). Warmth is communicated primarily through nonverbal behavior. A touch, a smile, a concerned look, or a particular tone of voice can all show a caring attitude. The very fact that an individual listens to another attentively with the whole presence demonstrates a valuing of the person (46).

Empathy is feeling with another. Dymond described it as "the imaginative transposing of oneself into the thinking, feeling, and acting of another, and so structuring the world as he does" (18). Although it is perhaps unrealistic to think that one individual can totally experience what another is thinking and feeling, the essence of empathy is attempting to understand parents from their perspective (22). The teacher can do this primarily by responding to parents in a way that lets them know that the teacher heard annd understood what they were trying to communicate — both content and affect. The response must not be a mechanical restatement, but a statement from a personal orientation that reflects the teacher's sincere effort to understand the individual parent (11, 22, 24).

Respect is based on a belief that parents have the capability to solve their own problems. As Hertel has stated, "Parents have the right and the duty to know about the child's progress in school. They also have the right to remain uninvolved if they so choose." (32). Respect is communicated by not denying the individual parent a particular perception of the child or of a problem. The fact that the parent's perspective may differ from the teacher's does not mean it is wrong, nor does it mean that the two cannot reach a mutual understanding. But judging or denying the parent's perception will most certainly have damaging effects (46). Respect also means not doing for parents what they can do for themselves; it means supporting them in their efforts. In short, respect communicates a collaborative rather than an authoritative or dependency relationship (10, 24).

These three conditions constitute the most basic elements of effective communication in conferencing, and they are the most necessary in the beginning stages of an interpersonal relationship. An effective level of these three conditions offered by the teacher will allow a meaningful exploration of the issues to occur and will help establish a sound base for the teacher-parent relationship characterized by a positive psychological climate of trust, caring, and respect (22, 25, 49, 57).

Concreteness is the ability to be specific in communicating. The teacher can be concrete by reinforcing parents' attempts to be specific in discussing their concerns or problems that relate to the conference goals. In this way the teacher demonstrates a willingness to help parents with their concerns regardless of positive or negative connotations (11, 24). According to Ostrom:

> Even a passing remark can trigger a chain of associations that generate intense and inappropriate feelings. Imagined insults have led to irreconcilable conflicts . . . . Effective communications require that one be courageous. It demands going to the front . . . the firing line, getting to where the action is. This allows for clarification, definition, and reconciliation of both imagined and real differences. (41)

This description reflects the meaning of concreteness. For the teacher this involves placing understanding above self-defense; seeking meaning for both parties to replace frustration, anger, or pessimism; and cutting through to the sources of these feelings. The teacher can communicate concreteness by clarifying as specifically as possible all that is essential in the matter under discussion (11, 22).

Genuineness is the teacher's ability to be real, to be congruent — not performing a role or dutifully carrying out a directive but involved with the parent(s) in an honest way. There must be a harmony between feelings, and verbal and nonverbal behavior. The teacher can communicate this quite simply by meaning what he/she says and saying what he/she means, still mindful of the best interest of all parties (22, 24).

Closely related to genuineness is *self-disclosure* (46). This is the ability to convey relevant personal experiences that the teacher feels may help parents realize that they are not alone with their problems or concerns, that others have had similar experiences and have found solutions. To be helpful, the teacher must be genuine in sharing the experiences and guard against shifting the focus of the conference from the parents' concerns to personal history (22, 24).

Immediacy is pointing out what is taking place between parent and teacher in the present relationship. It is threatening because of its present focus on the parties involved in the conference. Prichard notes that it is not surprising, therefore, to find parents arriving for conferences already feeling defensive" (43). Parents may exhibit a range of feelings and attitudes directed not toward the problem or conference topic but toward the teacher. This happens for a number of reasons. For example, the parent may be afraid of failing in some task with the child, and thus gives way to frustration and anger. Fearing that in the conference the teacher may discover these self-doubts, the parent attacks the teacher on a personal level. The teacher can communicate immediacy by pointing out this personal aspect of the conference (24).

Confrontation is pointing out discrepancies between enacted and verbal behaviors, self- and ideal concepts, insight and action, potential and present behaviors (24, 46). It can be the most threatening element of communication and must therefore be used with caution only after the teacher has established a positive environment (22, 24). If used correctly, confrontation can lead to growth, change, and problem solving (43, 58). Positive aspects should be stressed in conferences — that is, pointing out discrepancies between what is and what could be, or one's potential (24, 57).

Skill Areas in Effective Communication

The incorporation of these conditions into a systematic interpersonal communication model constitutes an effective parent-teacher conference intervention scheme (43, 49, 50, 54). According to Brown et al., the model is fundamentally neo-person-centered, tracing its origins to Carl Rogers's work in counseling and therapy (10). At present, however, the range and scope of the model is eclectic. Wilson notes that such a model of interpersonal communication seeks to establish and maintain a relationship with the parent, and, on the

13

strength of that relationship, facilitate movement from exploration to understanding to change, problem solving, or other appropriate goals (58). This is done through the skills of listening, attending, perceiving, responding, and initiating.

Listening forms the foundation of all interpersonal communication models. Most people feel that if nothing else, listening is something they can do well, but research indicates otherwise (16, 46). Adults are typically involved in communicative activities for 70 percent of the day. Of this amount, they spend 32 percent talking, 15 percent reading, 11 percent writing, and 42 percent listening (16). Even with so much practice, DeVito notes that "in actual practice most of us are relatively poor listeners and our listening behaviors could be made more effective and more efficient" (16). Effective listening is not a passive process but an active one that requires hard work and concentration (57). A number of specific reasons have been identified as to why listening is not as effective as it should be. Teachers who wish to make parent-teacher conferences more effective will find these reasons most helpful and will think of possible ways to overcome them when listening to parents.

First is the attitude with which one listens. If one views the parent as an infringement of the educational process rather than as an integral part of it, then listening is difficult and usually less than adequate (46). Second, when listening to others, listeners often make the mistake of concentrating on what they wish to say rather than on what the speaker is saying. In such cases, a list may help. A related situation, and even more difficult to deal with effectively, is listening to only part of what the speaker is saying. For example, a parent may be halfway through talking when he or she hits a nerve or sparks an idea that the teacher wishes to respond to, and rather than continuing to listen to the end the teacher is formulating a response. The real danger is that the end of the message may change the context of what was said earlier, thus making the listener's response inappropriate or unneeded, yet the listener failed to hear that part of the message (46). It has been demonstrated that most people respond to another's communication before they have had the opportunity physiologically to decode the entire communication (16).

A third pitfall is letting the mind drift off to other concerns while appearing to listen. Perhaps everyone has mastered this technique for self-survival — to escape from the boring oratory of someone droning on and on, for example. This is a real drawback in the conference, however, if the teacher wishes to effect mutual understanding. It may be helpful to identify some of the reasons for mind wandering in order to avoid them in the parent interview:

1. *Insufficient time.* Allow enough time for the conference so that the next commitment is not too pressing.

2. *Distractions.* Avoid physical settings that may be distracting; avoid times that may be distracting (such as the last hour before Christmas break begins).

A fourth concern is prejudging the individual or his/her intent. It is difficult to listen and really hear what a person is saying if one thinks one has heard it before or if the person turns one off (46). Related to this concern is self-understanding and the filter one listens through. Every teacher hears things that are filtered through personal experience, beliefs, and background. For example, "If he gives you any trouble, just hit him." Such a statement may turn a teacher off to the parents because of the teacher's values. As a result, the teacher's ability to work with the parents to help them develop more effective ways to deal with the child will be diminished. Thus the teacher must not suspend listening because of the content of a parent's message or its effect on him or her (22, 46).

When teachers listen actively, they listen not only with their ears but with their eyes and, in fact, with their whole being (57). This aspect of listening is a part of attending skills.

Attending skills are related to the physical aspects of listening and valuing the individual. By facial expression, eye contact, physical touch, voice tone, and gestures the teacher receives as well as sends many messages. "In effect the teacher is saying, because you are a person of worth and value I give you my complete attention. My physical being is focused on you." (57). Under such circumstances the teacher provides eye contact, facial expression, and a tone of voice appropriate to the emotional level of the conference, and a presence, not separated by artificial barriers such as desks, that physically says to the parent, "I care and I am listening." Physical touching, such as a handshake, an arm around the shoulder, a pat on the back, may be appropriate depending on circumstances and socially acceptable norms. Several studies have demonstrated the importance of touching (24). To realize the importance of attending in the communicating process, one need only recall talking about a serious concern to a person staring out the window at far-off places and playing with a paper clip.

"Perceiving differs from listening and attending in that listening and attending involve collecting all the cues that the [parent] provides — words, meanings, tones, expressions and gestures from an intellectual standpoint, whereas perceiving is bringing all the cues to personal awareness in an attempt to comprehend . . ." (22). Perceiving skills focus on understanding all that the individual has attempted to communicate — words, feelings, meanings, and emotions. Understanding

what is communicated is perhaps the most difficult of all communication skills: "Understanding another is not simple. It is something of a reciprocal process of understanding self, understanding the other, and being understandable." (41). The latter part of this thought from Ostrom bridges the gap from perceiving to responding skills.

Responding is the culmination of the three previous skill areas. To respond most effectively, the teacher must first be aware of and responsive to the affective meaning, the content, the nonverbal cues, and the emotional level of all that precedes the response (24). A response must convey that the teacher heard and understood what the parent said at the deepest level. It should not imply what is not there or go beyond the intent of the parent's statement; nor should it be more shallow than the parent's statement.

Initiating skills aid the teacher to summarize effectively, state goals clearly, enter into collaborative problem solving, or identify appropriate courses of action (24).

Application in Effective Communication

Before examining some of the most common roadblocks to effective communication, it may be helpful to give some examples of the application of these conditions and skills, paraphrased from several different sources (24, 43, 46).

Parent: (With eyes downcast, hands nervously interwined, and voice tentative) I'm never sure if I have really helped Gary with his schoolwork. I have so little time at home since I started working.

Teacher: The time pressure makes you feel a little doubtful about how effective your help really is since you have so little time to be with him.

Taking in all the cues provided, the teacher perceives the doubt the parent is experiencing. Perhaps beneath are feelings of guilt or inadequacy, but these are only tentative hypotheses and go beyond the actual communication. Understanding both the content of the message and the emotions then, the teacher responds —

Communicating warmth by listening to all that the parent said, and, it is presumed, facing the parent with an expression of interest and using an appropriate tone of voice.

Expressing empathy by attempting to understand and by accurately reflecting both the content and affective elements of the parent's statement.

Communicating respect by what is unsaid: "I think quality is more important than quantity." True or not, such a statement would deny the parent's right to personal misgivings, to a perception of the current dilemma. It is easy to argue that such a statement might be encouraging, but it neither helps the parent deal with the cause of the concern nor helps her move toward resolution. The teacher also communicates respect by not taking on the task, by not saying, for example, "Maybe I can work with Gary a little bit after school." This may be a part of a conventional collaborative solution; but here it is important that the teacher not take on a problem that is not hers or indirectly tell the parent, "You can't handle it, so I will."

Let us now assume that the parent's statement occurs after the teacher has had an opportunity to work with the parent for a while and the teacher knows some additional circumstances. A positive confrontation:

> *Teacher:* The time factor still bothers you, but Gary's work has been much improved the times he has said you were able to help.

This response still recognizes that the parent has doubts but confronts them on the basis of observable data. It is a positive rather than a negative confrontation. Other possible responses:

> *Teacher:* When Gary hasn't had help, he does poorly.

> or

> He always does well, you just worry too much.

An expression of immediacy may be warranted if the parent has added to the communication, "I certainly don't have time to waste here." To the teacher's original response might be added "and you're wondering if I can really be of any real assistance." Confrontation and immediacy can be a threat to both parties, but without them often no real progress is possible. Teachers must be willing to take such risks after first being sure to have listened and provided an environment where warmth, empathy, and respect dominate. In most conferences they will not have to go beyond these three basic conditions, but in some cases more may be necessary (49).

The final phase of helping parents deal with issues raised in parent-teacher conferences involves intitiating skills. These include summarizing, problem identification, and goal setting. Assuming that the teacher in the preceding example has established a basis of mutual understanding with the parent, an appropriate initiating statement would be:

> *Teacher:* Your greatest concern is that the time you spend with Gary be of the highest quality. Since you work, it is very difficult to feel that enough time is available for all that is required of you with Gary, the other kids, the job, the house, and so on. We share a concern over

Gary's current school performance and we both want more for him than he is currently giving. Together perhaps we can develop some activities for Gary that take little monitoring but let us both keep tabs on his progress.

This particular example demonstrates both summarization and goal setting. It is important to remember that one does not abandon the previous conditions of warmth, empathy and respect and go on to higher order skills when initiating solutions. When initiating, active listening, attending, and perceiving are still necessary (22).

Roadblocks to Effective Communication

The roadblocks to effective communications are numerous. Some have described one group of them as the dirty dozen (27, 41). These include commands, threats, preaching, lecturing, judging, and name-calling — behaviors that usually block comunication. Several general categories are prying, judging, glossing, denying, and escaping or pushing off (46). When a teacher asks many questions, particularly closed questions, the conference can be less than productive (22, 24). Parents will share what is comfortable for them to share given the current relationship between them and the teacher. Prying makes people feel uncomfortable and they may try to avoid the one who pries in the future (46). If questions must be asked, they should be as open as possible: "Questions that begin with *could, what,* and *show* tend to be more open-ended" (43).

Another roadblock to avoid is communicating a negative judgment about parents' behavior or attitudes. It is perhaps not possible to be nonjudgmental in the sense of being neutrally affected by those around one, but it is possible to suspend communicating judgments, particularly in the beginning. The key seems to be to value the worth of all people to be heard. Trust must precede and accompany any judgment or confrontation (24).

A third major roadblock to effective parent-teacher communication is a tendency to gloss over problems or deny that they exist. Teachers are in the profession because they want to help others. Sometimes it is painful to deal with the problems of others or to see and experience their fears, anxieties, and turmoil. Statements such as "It can't be that bad." or "Things are bound to get better." are no substitute for dealing with issues that must be faced to find real solutions (46).

Often some concerns shared by parents in the conference may make the teacher uncomfortable on a personal level. Perhaps the teacher feels inadequate to deal with the problem or the content and ignores it, trying to escape or push it off, or the teacher does not have the expertise to solve it. But if a problem is related to the goals of the conference, it should be dealt with, however unpleasant (8, 41).

This has been a brief review of the interpersonal communication skills demonstrated to be most effective for teachers in the parent-teacher conference or similar-type interactions. The research for the effectiveness of such skills is exhaustive. In the educational setting alone, these skills have been demonstrated to improve the school climate, teacher-teacher communication, teacher-student relationships, and teacher-parent relationships (3, 10, 25, 51, 53). Teacher training in these skills has led to fewer disruptive problems and increased school achievement, student self-concept, and teacher self-concept (4, 31, 37, 53). Teachers have reported increased satisfaction with their skills in the classroom and have been judged more effective by others (4, 6). It has also been demonstrated that teachers can learn these skills and apply them to a number of different settings including the parent-teacher conference (4, 43, 47, 59).

Developing Effective Communication Skills

Teachers can acquire effective communication skills in different ways. Some have acquired them through models in learning situations (3, 50); most educators, however, must set out to learn how to be effective in interpersonal communication. Among the resources available, the most effective seems to be a training group led by an individual who has a high degree of mastery (12, 22). Such a group allows for modeling, practice, and a safe environment to unlearn roadblocks and acquire new modes of communicating (24, 45). For those who do not have the opportunity to work with a training group, several books are available. They include *Human Relations Development: A Manual for Educators* (22) and *The Skills of Teaching: Interpersonal Skills* (11). These works attempt to provide a systematic guide to learning the skills of interpersonal communication.

Human interactions such as those represented in the parent-teacher conference can have a positive influence on the course of education. As the professional member of this team, the teacher has a responsibility to assume the burden not for the outcome, but of assuring that the encounter be as productive as possible. Interpersonal communication skills form the base of success or failure in this endeavor. In spite of many roadblocks to effectiveness, a set of conditions and skills known to promote success can be learned and can provide positive results for children, parents, and teachers.

THE PARENT-TEACHER CONTACT*

Interpersonal communication skills can be effectively applied whether the parent contact is formal or informal. Informal contacts are those times other than during a scheduled appointment when the teacher meets with parents. They include being stopped by a parent in the hall before or after school or over refreshments at the PTA meeting, or sending a note home with the child. Formal contacts are those scheduled in advance, whether teacher- or parent-initiated. The main difference between these two kinds of contacts is the amount of preparation time. The spontaneity of the informal contact and the advance notice of the formal contact create special characteristics which are addressed later in this publication.

Conferences are usually parent- or teacher-initiated, although there may be times when the student or another adult initiates the meeting. Teacher- and parent-initiated conferences have unique characteristics as well as elements common to both.

Finally, the nature of the conference may differ depending upon the age and grade level of the child. Generally, parents are more involved in their child's education during the early years; at the high school level the student is given more responsibility for his or her educational development. Regardless of student age and grade level, the characteristics of effective parent-teacher interactions remain the same.

Conference Characteristics

Parent: I just wanted to stop by and tell you how much we appreciate all the effort you are putting into teaching David math this year. He hated math last year, but is so excited about the things you are doing in class. I know math can be a difficult subject to make exciting. But you've triggered something in David.

What a delight to hear. It certainly would be a joy if all parent contacts were so gratifying. By requesting conferences for positive reasons from time to time, teachers can encourage such parental contacts.

Parent: This is the third time I've had to come in to this school this year. I've had to take off work — and lost a half day's pay. Each time it's been because of this child's problems. What is it this time?

*Portions of this section are adapted with permission from "The Parent-Teacher Conference" by E. H. Robinson and J. C. Rotter. In *The ABC's of Classroom Discipline,* edited by L. Baruth and D. Eckstein. Dubuque, Iowa: Kendall Hunt, 1982.

This may not be a typical parental statement, but at least one teacher has experienced it. Under ideal conditions, teachers would never hear such negative utterances. However, reality guarantees at least occasional negative reactions. Nevertheless, this type of response can be reduced through advance planning and effective communication skills. If and when such reactions become reality, a skillful approach to the upset parent can result in a harmonious resolution.

One of the greatest compliments that a teacher can receive is a request from a parent for a conference. Unfortunately, formal parental contacts are often avoided, — at the expense of the child — because either the parent or the teacher feels apprehensive or inadequate.

> *Parent:* I'm concerned about Beth's grades in social studies. She's always been a good student, but something isn't going right in this class. I wonder if you can give me any ideas why she's doing so poorly?

In a nondefensive but concerned manner, this parent is seeking help from the teacher. The statement suggests a collaborative effort to help the child overcome a given academic problem. Again, this is an ideal situation. But when a sincere request for help comes, it is important that the teacher be prepared to respond in a facilitative way.

Common Elements of Conferences

When possible, and especially if it is the parent's first visit, *meet the parent* at the school office or building entry. Nothing is more distracting and frustrating for a visitor than wandering around corridors trying to find the right classroom. To an outsider all rooms look alike.

One of the major complaints from both teachers and parents is that there is not enough time to do everything that needs to be done. This is perhaps the major lament about life itself. But rushing parents through a conference can be both frustrating and counterproductive. A little extra time taken for the conference itself can considerably reduce the followup time needed to correct any misunderstandings created by rushing in the first place. According to the adage, there's never enough time to do something right, but always enough time to do it over again. One critical element in effective parent conferences, then, is to *allow enough time*.

A related issue — the changing roles of people in the world of work and the increasing number of families with two working parents — can make scheduling some conferences more difficult. One solution to this problem is to ask parents at the beginning of the year for convenient times for conferences. If both parents are unavailable for daytime conferences because of their working schedules, perhaps some compensatory time arrangements can be made for teachers to meet them in the evening. Other options are certainly available. Usually a bit of creative discussion between the school and the parents can overcome these problems. The point is to make every effort to provide time for meaningful interactions between parents and teachers.

Depending upon the issues and the teacher's professional judgment of the impact upon the child, the teacher must decide whether the child would benefit from being present during the conference. Generally speaking, it is recommended that since the child is the focus of the conference, he/she should be present to take full part and to benefit from the interaction. Furthermore, why make something, which has the child as its focus, such a mystery to the child?

Another element, at times the most difficult, is to *keep an open mind* about what the parents are communicating and avoid becoming defensive.

Listening is the teacher's best tool. By encouraging the parents to convey their concerns and hearing all the explicit and implicit messages, the teacher can be in the best position to respond in a facilitative manner. Listen to the words, the way they are presented, and the acompanying mannerisms to be certain to hear not only the words, but the intended message. The words themselves convey only a small amount of the message.

If at any time you are uncertain as to the message the parent is conveying, *ask for clarification* as soon possible. Confusion can compound itself very quickly and lead to misunderstandings, misjudgments, and ill-designed solutions.

Avoid overwhelming the parent with the presence of nonessential school personnel. Too many people can provoke defensiveness, if not fear, in the parent. It is important to remember that the conference may be a very stressful experience for the parent. In some cases, it may, however, be necessary to have witnesses or someone with special knowledge or skills present. If so, avoid overwhelming the parent verbally or nonverbally. If the parent appears exceptionally uneasy, it may be necessary to make some adjustment or ask the parent what seems to be troublesome.

Educational jargon can be confusing and insulting to parents. Avoid terms such as "criterion-referenced testing," "personality characteristics," and "least restrictive environment." Refer to specific concerns and use terms that are clear to parents to prevent misunderstandings. The parent-teacher conference should be a collaborative event; when parents do not understand the terms, it becomes one-sided (33).

Remain poised. Show parents *respect* and concern — respect

for them as persons and concern for them as patrons of the school — maintaining a professional demeanor at all times.

Be sure that the environment for the conference is conducive to open communication. *Avoid physical barriers* such as desks or counters between teacher and parent. Choose a comfortable place in the classroom or school building where interruptions are unlikely.

When concluding the conference, *part on a positive note.* Whenever possible, save at least one positive comment about the student, the school, and/or the parent for the end. If necessary, arrange for followup conferences or referral procedures before the parent leaves, and be certain to carry out any promised followup.

When to Have Conferences

Ideally, all parent-teacher conferences would concern positive events. Realistically, however, many conferences are called because something is going awry. Teachers should by all means follow through on these problem areas. It is a good idea, however, for teachers to surprise themselves and perhaps the student and the parent by having more conferences for positive rather than negative events. Such conferences can offset the negative ones and can thus be a relief from the can offset the negative ones and can thus be a relief from the stressful nature of the latter. They can also help develop a mind set with parents and students that someone cares when things are going well.

Figure 1, the Effective Conferencing Scale, is offered to help teachers become aware of their approach to parent conferences. Simply place a checkmark in the appropriate column after each item. Teachers who check "Always" on all 10 items are probably having success in their interactions with parents. Consistency is a critical factor. Those who check "Sometimes" or "Never" on some items may have a clue to problems that occur during parent conferences. After their next parent conference they may want to refer to the scale and rate themselves again.

The scale items summarize some of the common elements of parent-teacher coferences whether parent- or teacher-initiated. Individual teachers can think of other elements.

The following pages discuss those elements unique to teacher-initiated conferences. They are in addition to the common elements just discussed.

Teacher-Initiated Conferences

When the teacher calls the conference, the burden of responsibility for its structure resides with the teacher. In these parent contacts openness and straightforwardness are essential, but in a facilitative manner.

Figure 1
Effective Conferencing Scale

	Always (2)	Sometimes (1)	Never (0)
1. Prepare for conference in advance.			
2. Give parent(s) some idea in advance of topic to be discussed.			
3. Allow enough time for conference.			
4. Avoid becoming defensive when parents question judgment.			
5. Maintain an open mind to parent ideas.			
6. Listen to all parent is saying (verbal and nonverbal) before responding.			
7. Avoid overwhelming parent(s) with presence of other school personnel.			
8. Avoid overwhelming parent(s) with irrelevant material or use of jargon.			
9. Avoid physical barriers such as desk, uncomfortable chairs.			
10. Follow up on commitments.			

> *Teacher:* Mr. Hope, you need to see me as soon as possible to discuss John's poor study habits.

What is wrong with this statement? First of all, the use of the word "you" implies that the parent has the problem and places the burden on him. Second, the urgency suggested in the statement can arouse undue anxiety. Third, the negative thrust (the use of the word "poor") suggests little hope for improvement and can easily be interpreted as an insult to the parent — after all, John is his own flesh and blood.

> *Teacher:* Mr. Hope, the reason I have called is to discuss with you how we might work together to improve John's study habits.

Notice in this case that the teacher suggests a collaborative effort with the parent, at the same time pointing out the source of the difficulty. In addition, the teacher implies through the statement that there is hope — the difficulty can be overcome.

If the initial contact is verbal, attempt to resolve the concern during the session if possible. If the nature of the concern requires the parent to have some lead time before discussion, then arrange for a conference. In any case, avoid the surprise attack. It may arouse anxiety and anger.

Prepare for the conference in advance. Do not allow a situation like the following to happen:

Teacher: Oh, hello Ms. . . . What was it we were to talk about?

Plan for the meeting by *listing the specific points to be made* and the questions to be raised. Take the time to plan ahead and much of the needless followup time will be reduced. In fact, as part of the advance planning it is helpful to prepare a *written progress report* to share with the parent that includes

1. A survey of student progress
2. Areas of concern
3. Areas of strength
4. A proposed plan of action, where appropriate.

When the parent arrives, structure the session for the parent. That is, explain the why, what, how, and when. It is helpful to both teacher and parent to have an agenda clearly outlining the purpose and procedure of the conference. Include time at the beginning for the parent to review and discuss the written progress report.

Although most teachers have regularly scheduled conferences with parents, especially in the early grades, it is important to deal with concerns as they arise. By waiting for the scheduled conference day, when time may be limited, the problem may compound itself. Immediacy without panic is the name of the game.

Finally, by all means avoid embarrassment by matching child with parent. If there are three Jacks in a class, be sure to talk about the right Jack.

These pointers, together with the common elements discussed earlier, will not guarantee a smooth conference but they should prevent many of the potential rough edges.

Parent-Initiated Conferences

Many times, more likely in the elementary grades, parents will request a conference.

Parent: I'd like to stop by to talk to you about Rhonda's work in social studies. She doesn't seem to understand the material.

or

Jay complains of stomach aches in the morning before school, especially on days when he's going to have a test. Can you tell me what to do?

Again, these are two examples from countless possibilities. It is not the intent of this section to discuss the cause-effect relationship of these incidents, but they are school-related concerns to the parents and therefore should be addressed. The question here is how to address them.

First of all, keep in mind the common elements of parent-teacher conferences discussed earlier. In addition, the following five elements will contribute to a smooth and successful conference.

As with teacher-initiated conferences, make certain to *positively identify the parent requesting the meeting*. Little can be more embarrassing to the teacher and disturbing to the parent than to match the wrong parent and child.

Second, if the parent shares the topic of concern in advance, *collect the necessary background information* to expedite a fruitful encounter. In the case of the parent who is concerned about her daughter's progress in social studies, be prepared to share with her the records of the student's classroom performance and any observations you have made that may help the parent, and perhaps yourself, better understand the situation. In the case of the student who complains of stomach aches, in addition to academic data, it may be advisable to consult the school counselor or nurse. Regardless of the concern, *have the pertinent student records accessible for the conference*.

As has been emphasized all along, during the conference invite the parents to fully express their concerns. *Do not make assumptions* before obtaining all the facts and impressions from the parents, and others when necessary. And, in keeping with this last element of parent-initiated conferences, be persistent in *getting the complete story* before suggesting any action or solution. Nothing can be more harmful than prescribing the wrong action — just as prescribing Maalox for test anxiety does not solve the real problem.

To summarize, then, whether initiated by parent or teacher, all conferences contain some common elements which enhance the potential for success. They also contain some elements that are unique to each type. Figure 2 summarizes these elements.

LEGAL AND ETHICAL CONSIDERATIONS

The interest of parents in the education of their children is not new. Parents have long desired that their children receive the best possible education; likewise teachers have been concerned to provide the best possible learning environment. Unfortunately, however, many judgments, although made in the best of interest of the child, have

Figure 2

Elements of Effective Parent-Teacher Conferences

Teacher-Initiated	*Common Elements*	*Parent-Initiated*
—Prepare for confer-ence in advance. —Give parent(s) some idea of topic. —Specify points to be made. —Prepare written progress report to include 1. Survey of student progress 2. Areas of concern 3. Areas of strength —Don't wait for regularly scheduled conference if a matter arises; deal with it. —Structure conference for parent(s): why, what, when; explain purpose. —Allow parent(s) time to read and/or discuss written summary.	—Allow enough time. —Determine whether student should be present. —Do not become defensive; maintain open mind. —Listen to all parent is saying, specifically and implied. —Seek clarification when necessary. —Avoid overwhelming parent with presence of nonessential school personnel. —Avoid overwhelming parent with irrelevant material or use of jargon; be thorough. —Meet parent(s) at building entry point if possible. —Show parent concern and respect — respect as person, concern as patron of school; maintain positive professional demeanor. —Make environment for conference conducive to open communication; avoid physical barriers. —Attempt to part on positive note; set up future conference or referral procedures before parent leaves. —Be sure to carry out any promised followup.	—Positively identify parent requesting meeting. —If parent shares topic, collect necessary background information. —Have pertinent student records accessible for conference. —Do not make assumptions; invite parents to express concerns. —Get complete story before suggesting action or solutions.

not necessarily been made with the input of all parties — teachers, parents, and, least of all, students.

In 1974 Congress passed the Family Educational Rights and Privacy Act, better known as the Buckley Amendment. In essence this law and its accompanying guidelines state that parents of minor students have ·

> . . . the right to inspect and review any and all official records, files and data directly related to their children, including all material that is incorporated into each student's cumulative record folder and intended for school use or to be available to parties outside the school or school system, and specifically including but not necessarily limited to identifying data, academic work completed, level of achievement (grades, standardized achievement scores), attendance data, scores of standardized intelligence, aptitude and psychological tests, interest inventory results, health data, family background information, teacher or counselor ratings and observations, and verified reports of serious recurrent behavior patterns. (26a)

In addition, Public Law 94-142, the Education for All Handicapped Children Act, passed in 1975, guarantees the right of all children, regardless of the extent of their handicap, to a free, appropriate education. This act calls for specific policies and procedures to be adopted by school districts to assure its implementation. Parents and teachers are key parts of the process.

Within the past decade, these two laws have perhaps had the greatest impact on the importance of frequent and effective parent-teacher conferences.

CONCLUSION

Many teachers would say that the one thing their training least prepares them to do is to conduct parent conferences (8). Effective parent-teacher conferences, however, have the potential to be the "single most educationally valuable event" for the student during the school year (44).

With increased parental involvement in the day-to-day operation of the schools and greater parental awareness of the educational process, it becomes apparent that educators need to be prepared to respond to the renewed parental interest in the education of their children. From both an ethical and a legal perspective, communication between parents and teachers is imperative.

Teachers can acquire communication skills for effective parent-teacher interactions and apply them in both formal and informal contacts. Listening, perceiving, attending, responding, and initiating skills can help reduce the roadblocks and anxieties apparent in many parent-teacher interactions. The core elements of effective conferencing identified in this publication, when applied with these basic communication skills in mind, can turn a potentially devastating experience into one that is rewarding for all concerned.

As educators are being asked to perform more and more tasks within the school setting, the parent-teacher conference is becoming a critical function of teacher effectiveness in many areas of their responsibility. As a result of the conference, parents can become an invaluable ally of teachers in their efforts to provide the best possible education for children by helping them focus on what is most important — the education and well-being of students.

BIBLIOGRAPHY

1. Alexander, R. N. "Evaluation Procedures in Parent-Teacher Conferencing." Paper presented at Annual International Convention of the Council for Exceptional Children, Atlanta, April 1977.
2. Anderson, L. W. *Assessing Affective Characteristics in the Schools*. Boston: Allyn and Bacon, 1981.
3. Aspy, D. N. *Toward a Technology for Humanizing Education*. Champaign, Ill.: Research Press, 1972.
4. ———, and Roebuck, F. N. *Kids Don't Learn from People They Don't Like*. Amherst, Mass.: Human Resource Development Press, 1977.
5. Berclay, G. J. *Parent Involvement in the Schools*. Washington, D.C.: National Education Association, 1977.
6. Berensen, D. "The Effects of Systematic Relations Training upon Classroom Performance of Elementary School Teachers." *Journal of Research and Development in Education* 4 (Winter 1971).
7. Birnie, B. "Working with Parents." *Instructor*, March 1980.
8. Black, K. N. "The Teacher and the Parent Conferences." *Contemporary Education*, Spring 1979.
9. Bloom, B. *Human Characteristics and School Learning*. New York: McGraw-Hill, 1976.
10. Brown, O.; Wyne, M.; Blackburn, J.; and Powell, W. C. *Consultation: Strategy for Improving Education*. Boston: Allyn and Bacon, 1979.
11. Carkhuff, R. R.; Berensen, D. H.; and Pierce, R. M. *The Skills of Teaching: Interpersonal Skills*. Amherst, Mass.: Human Resource Development Press, 1976.
12. ———, and Beirman, R. "Training as a Preferred Mode of Treatment of Parents of Emotionally Disturbed Children." *Journal of Counseling Psychology*, 1970.
13. Catterall, C. D., and Gazda, G. M. *Strategies for Helping Students*. Springfield, Ill.: Charles C. Thomas, 1978.
14. Colleta, A. J. *Working Together: A Guide to Parent Development*. Atlanta: Humanics Press, 1977.
15. Crowe, R. "The Traditional Family Myth." *Carolina Counselor*, Spring 1981.
16. DeVito, J. A. *The Interpersonal Communication Book*. New York: Harper and Row, 1976.
17. Dinkmeyer D., and McKay, G. *Systematic Training for Effective Parenting*. Circle Pines, Minn.: American Guidance Service, 1976.
18. Dymond, R. F. "A Preliminary Investigation of the Relation of Insight and Empathy." *Journal of Consulting Psychology* 12 (July-August 1948).
19. Featherstone, J. "Family Matters." *Harvard Educational Review*, February 1979.
20. Foshay, A. J. "The Problem of Community." In *New Views of School and Community*, edited by P. Markum. Washington, D.C.: Association for Childhood Education International, 1973.
21. Gazda, G. M. "Systematic Human Relations Training in Teacher Preparation and Inservice Education." *Journal of Research and Development in Education* 4 (Winter 1971).
22. ———; Asbury, F. R.; Balzer, F. J.; Childers, W. C.; and Walters, R. P. *Human Relations Development: A Manual for Educators*. Boston: Allyn and Bacon, 1977.
23. ———; Childers, W. C.; and Walters, R. P. *Human Relations Development: A Manual for Health Services*. Boston: Allyn and Bacon, 1979.
24. ———; Duncan, J. A.; Maples, M. F.; and Brown, J. L. *The Heart of Teaching: Applications Handbook*. Bloomington, Ind.: Agency for Instructional Television, 1976.
25. ———; Robinson, E. H.; Wilson, E. S.; and Schumacher, R. *"Affective/ Interpersonal Communication Skills Development Model for Educators: Its Slope and Impact."* Paper presented at meeting of American Personnel and Guidance Association, Washington, D.C., March 1978.
26. Gesslein, C. H. "Teacher-Parent Report Conferences for Moderately and Severely Mentally Retarded Children and Youth: A Guide for Teachers." EDRS 065 149, July 1971.

26a. Getson, R., and Schweid, R. "School Counselors and the Buckley Amendment — Ethical Standards Squeeze." *School Counselor* 24 (September 1976): 57.
27. Gordon, I. J., and Breivogel, W. *Building Effective Home-School Relationships.* Boston: Allyn and Bacon, 1977.
28. Gordon, T. *Teacher Effectivness Training.* New York: Peter H. Wyden, 1974.
29. Halas, L. "Working with Parents." *Instructor,* March 1978.
30. Harbach, R. L., and Asbury, F. R. "Some Effects of Empathic Understanding on Negative Student Behaviors. *Humanist Educator,* Spring 1976.
31. Hefele, T. J. "The Effects of Systematic Human Relations Training upon Student Achievement." *Journal of Research and Development in Education* 4 (Winter 1971).
32. Hertel, S. M. "A Study of Parent Attitudes on the Parent Teacher Conference." EDRS 147 288, May 1977.
33. Kline, S. D. "Parent-School Conferences: Guidelines and Objectives." *Exceptional Parent,* August 1979.
34. Kopple, H., and Conner, K. *The Mastery Learning Manual.* Philadelphia: School District of Philadelphia, 1980.
35. Kroth, R. L., and Simpson, R. *Parent Conferences: A Teaching Strategy.* Denver: Love Publication Co., in press.
36. Long, A. "Facing the Stress of Parent-Teacher Conferences." *Today's Education,* September/October 1976.
37. Losen, S. M., and Diament, B. *Parent Conferences in the Schools.* Boston: Allyn and Bacon, 1978.
38. Millar, T. P. "When Parents Talk to Teachers." *Elementary School Journal,* May 1969.
39. Morris, R. L. "Thunder on the Right: Past and Present." *Education,* Winter 1978.
40. Murphy, S. "A Successful Parent-School Relationship." Proceedings of Workshop on Parent Involvement, EDRS 160 182, Summer 1972.
41. Ostrom, G. "Establishing Effective Communications Between Parents and Teachers." Proceedings of Workshop on Parent Involvement, EDRS 160 182, Summer 1972.
42. Pedrini, D. T.; Pedrini, B. C.; Egnoski, E. J.; Heater, J. D.; and Nelson, M. D. "Pre-, Post- and Follow-up Testing of Teacher Effectiveness Training." *Education* (Spring 1976).
43. Prichard, K. K. "Effective Parent-Teacher Conferences in Urban Schools." ERIC Document ED 152942, 1977.
44. Rabbitt, J. A. "The Parent/Teacher Conference: Trauma or Teamwork?" *Phi Delta Kappan,* March 1978.
45. Robinson, E. H. "Effects of Teacher Interpersonal Communication Skills Training on Measures of Teacher Self-Esteem and Student Achievement." Paper presented at University of South Carolina Conference on Educational Research, December 1980.
46. ———. "The Interpersonal Skills of Teaching." In *The ABC's of Classroom Discipline,* edited by L. Baruth and D. Eckstein. Dubuque, Iowa: Kendall Hunt, 1982.
47. ———, and Brosh, M. C. "Communication Skills Training for Resource Teachers." *Journal of Learning Disabilities,* March 1980.
48. ———, and Robinson, S. L. "Early Childhood Programs: A Planning Priority." *Childhood Education,* November/December 1981.
49. ———, and Rotter, J C. "The Parent-Teacher Conference." In *The ABC's of Classroom Discipline,* edited by L. Baruth and D. Eckstein. Dubuque, Iowa: Kendall Hunt, 1982.
50. ———, and ———. "The Parent-Teacher Relationship." Paper presented at University of South Carolina Conference on Educational Research, November 1981.
51. ———, and Wilson, E. S. "Effects of Human Relations Training on Indices of Skill Development and Self-Concept Change of Classroom Teachers." *Journal for Specialists in Group Work,* July 1980.
52. Saba, R. G. "Effectiveness of Human Relations Training for Undergraduate Proctors in a Mystery-Based Course." *Humanist Educator* (December 1975).

53. ———, "The Effects of Unsolicited Attention on Frequency of Misbehavior in Grade Levels K-Postsecondary." *Humanist Educator* (September 1977).
54. Stoffer, D. L. "An Investigation of Positive Behavior Changes as a Function of Genuineness, Non-Possessive Warmth, and Empathetic Understanding." *Journal of Educational Research* 63 (January 1970).
55. Swick, K. J.; Duff, R. E.; and Hobson, C. F. *Parent Involvement: Strategies for Early Childhood Educators.* Champaign, Ill.: Stipes Publishing Co., 1981.
56. Tyack, D. B. *Turning Points in American Educational History.* Waltham, Mass.: Blaisdell Publishing Co., 1967.
57. Webster, E., and Ward, L. "Developing Communication Skills." Proceedings of Workshop on Parent Involvement, EDRS 160 182, Summer 1972.
58. Wilson, E. S. "The Effects of an Inservice HRT Model on the Self-Concept of Elementary School Teachers." Doctoral Dissertation, Duke University, 1979.
59. ———, and Robinson, E. H. "The Generalizability of Human Relations Training." University of Montvallo, 1981.

SELECTED RESOURCES (Revised)

Barron, B. G., and Colvin, J. M. "Teacher-Talk to Parents." *Education* 105 (Fall 1984): 76–78.

Conroy, M. T. "Parent-Teacher Conferences (Tips for Industrial Arts Teachers)." *Industrial Education* 71 (April 1982): 37–38.

Ellenburg, F. C., and Lanier, N. J. "Interacting Effectively with Parents." *Childhood Education* 60 (May/June 1984): 315–18.

Fredericks, A. D., et al. "How to Talk to Parents and Get the Message Home." *Instructor* 93 (November/December 1983): 64–66+.

Gerrity, K. "Dear Mrs. McCrea, About That Conference Next Week." *Learning* 11 (February 1983): 46–47.

Gress, J. R., and Carroll, M. E. "Parent-Professional Partnership—and the IEP." *Academic Therapy* 20 (March 1985): 443–49.

Heinrich, L. B. "Parent/Teacher Conferences: Include the Student, Please." *Learning* 85 14 (October 1985): 86–87.

Hoemann, V., and Gronemeyer, R. "Summit Savvy: How to Have an Effective Parent Conference." *Instructor* 92 (October 1982): 38.

Hoover, T., and Hoover, J. "Enhancing the Parent-Teacher Conference with the Microcomputer." *Educational Technology* 23 (March 1983): 23–31.

Judge, L. "Scheduling Conferences? I Couldn't Get to First Base!" *Instructor* 92 (April 1983): 18.

Lee, H. C. "Productive Parent-Teacher Conferences." *Educational Horizons* 61 (Fall 1982): 25+.

Lockavitch, J. F., Jr. "'Parent'—Remember This Word Before a Difficult Conference." *Academic Therapy* 19 (November 1983): 199–203.

Manning, B. H. "Conducting a Worthwhile Parent-Teacher Conference." *Education* 105 (Summer 1985): 342–48.

Manning, M. L. "The Involved Father: A New Challenge in Parent Conferences." *Clearing House* 57 (September 1983): 17–19.

———. "The Involved Father and Parent-Teacher Conferences." *Education Digest* 49 (April 1984): 52–54.

McSweeney, J. P. "Five Guidelines for Parent-Teacher Conferences." *Clearing House* 56 (March 1983): 319–20.

Price, B. J., and Marsh, G. E. "Practical Suggestions for Planning and Conducting Parent Conferences." *Teaching Exceptional Children* 17 (Summer 1985): 274–78.